The Fearless Entrepreneur:

Transforming Anxiety Into Action

A combination of passion and perseverance for a first time entrepreneur

Zaytoona Nur

Table of Contents

Chapter 1

Embracing Fear as Fuel

Understanding Fear in Entrepreneurship

Fear is an intrinsic part of the entrepreneurial journey, often lurking in the shadows as we pursue our dreams. It can manifest in various forms: fear of failure, fear of judgment, or even fear of success. Understanding this complex emotion is the first thing towards transforming it from a paralysing force into a powerful catalyst for growth. Entrepreneurs must recognise that fear is not the enemy; rather, it is a signal that pushes us to confront challenges, take risks, and ultimately evolve. By reframing our perspective on fear, we can harness its energy to propel us forward instead of holding us back.

Every successful entrepreneur has encountered fear, yet it is how they respond to it that sets them apart. Consider the story of a young woman who launched her own tech startup despite having no prior experience in the industry. She was terrified of the possibility of failure and the scrutiny that would come with it. However, instead of allowing fear to dictate her actions, she chose to embrace it. She understood that every great achievement comes with uncertainty. By leaning into her fear, she transformed it into motivation, leading her to seek out mentors, gather knowledge, and build a supportive network that ultimately contributed to her success.

There is also the inspiring tale of a seasoned entrepreneur who faced a significant downturn in his business. Initially, he was paralysed by the fear of losing everything he had worked for. However, instead of succumbing to despair, he took a step back to analyse the situation. This pause allowed him to confront his fear head-on. He realised that failure was not the end but a lesson in resilience. By innovating and pivoting his business model, he not only survived but emerged stronger, demonstrating that fear can lead to profound insights and transformative change when we choose to face it.

Moreover, fear often stems from our innate desire for safety and security. In entrepreneurship, the road is seldom predictable, which can intensify anxiety. However, embracing this uncertainty can lead to unexpected opportunities. An entrepreneur who initially feared taking risks may find that stepping outside of their comfort zone opens doors to new partnerships, markets, and ideas. By understanding that discomfort is part of the growth process, they can reframe their mindset, viewing challenges as stepping stones rather than obstacles. This shift can unlock creativity and innovation, key ingredients for entrepreneurial success.

Finally, cultivating a community of support can significantly alleviate the burdens of fear in entrepreneurship. Surrounding oneself with like-minded individuals who share their struggles and triumphs fosters a sense of belonging and encouragement. Listening to the success stories of others who have faced their fears can inspire action and resilience in overcoming personal anxieties. By sharing experiences, entrepreneurs can learn from one another, realising that they are not alone in their fears. This collective strength not only empowers individuals but also creates an environment where fear is acknowledged and transformed into a shared journey of growth and accomplishment.

The Power of Vulnerability

The journey of entrepreneurship is often laden with fear and uncertainty, creating an environment where vulnerability can feel like a weakness. However, embracing vulnerability can become one of the most powerful tools in an entrepreneur's armoury. When we allow ourselves to be open about our fears, struggles, and failures, we not only humanise our experiences but also create authentic connections with others. This authenticity fosters a supportive community, where shared stories of overcoming adversity can inspire and uplift, transforming our fears into stepping stones for success.

Many successful entrepreneurs have faced moments of intense vulnerability. Take the story of a startup founder who, after multiple failed attempts, found the courage to share his struggles with his audience. Instead of hiding behind a façade of success, he opened up about the fear of failure that kept him awake at night. This honesty resonated with many aspiring entrepreneurs, creating a bond based on shared experiences. By revealing his vulnerabilities, he not only garnered support but also gained valuable insights from others who had walked similar paths, turning his fear into a catalyst for growth and innovation.

Vulnerability also encourages a mindset shift that is essential in entrepreneurship. When we confront our fears instead of avoiding them, we begin to see them as opportunities for learning. Each challenge becomes a lesson, each setback a stepping stone. This perspective allows us to approach our ventures with resilience and creativity. By acknowledging our vulnerabilities, we become more adaptable and open to feedback, which can lead to innovative solutions and new paths going forward. In this way, vulnerability is not just about admitting fear; it is about harnessing that fear to fuel our passion and drive.

Furthermore, vulnerability fosters an environment of collaboration and support among peers. Entrepreneurs who embrace their own fears often create spaces where others feel safe to do the same. This leads to the sharing of ideas, resources, and strategies that can help everyone involved. When we cultivate a culture of vulnerability within our networks, we encourage collective growth rather than competition. In this nurturing environment, entrepreneurs can thrive, bolstered by the strength of their community and the shared determination to overcome challenges together.

Ultimately, the power of vulnerability lies in its ability to transform fear into action. When we accept our fears and share our authentic selves, we unlock the potential for personal and professional growth. Vulnerability invites empathy, connection, and understanding, turning what is often seen as a weakness into a powerful force for change. As entrepreneurs, embracing vulnerability can lead us not only to greater success in our ventures but also to a deeper understanding of ourselves and the impact we can make in the world. By transforming anxiety into action through vulnerability, we pave the way for a fearless entrepreneurial journey.

Shifting Perspectives: From Fear to Opportunity

In the journey of entrepreneurship, fear often looms large, casting shadows over our dreams and ambitions. It can manifest as self-doubt, the fear of failure, or the anxiety of stepping into the unknown. However, the most successful entrepreneurs have learned to shift their perspectives, transforming fear into a catalyst for opportunity. By reframing fear as a natural part of the process, they unlock doors that once seemed closed. This shift in mindset is not just a theory; it is a proven strategy that can lead to personal growth and business success.

Consider the story of a young entrepreneur who faced overwhelming doubt as she launched her business. Every day was a battle against the nagging voice that whispered, "What if you fail?" Instead of succumbing to this fear, she chose to confront it head-on. She began to see her anxiety not as a barrier but as a signal, guiding her toward areas that needed attention and improvement. Each moment of fear became an opportunity for learning, allowing her to re-evaluate her business model and develop resilience. This transformation enabled her to not only survive but thrive in a competitive landscape.

Another inspiring example comes from a seasoned business owner who faced a major setback during an economic downturn. Initially paralysed by fear and uncertainty, he eventually realised that within this challenge lay a unique chance to innovate. Instead of clinging to outdated practices, he shifted his focus to emerging trends and customer needs that were evolving in response to the crisis. By embracing the fear of change, he was able to pivot his business strategy, leading to new revenue streams and revitalised growth. This experience taught him that fear can be a powerful motivator for adaptation and creativity.

The art of shifting perspectives from fear to opportunity is not merely about individual stories; it's a collective journey that many entrepreneurs embark upon. It requires a conscious effort to cultivate a mindset that embraces challenges as stepping stones rather than stumbling blocks.

This mindset encourages a culture of experimentation, where failure is seen not as the end, but as a valuable lesson that propels one forward. When entrepreneurs share their fears and the subsequent breakthroughs, they inspire others to do the same, creating a supportive community where collective growth thrives.

Ultimately, the transition from fear to opportunity is a profound shift that can redefine one's entrepreneurial path. It invites individuals to embrace vulnerability, knowing that it is often the precursor to significant breakthroughs. By acknowledging fear and using it as a driving force, anyone can transform their entrepreneurial journey into a meaningful adventure. As we learn to harness the power of fear, we open ourselves to a world of possibilities, where every challenge is an opportunity waiting to be seized.

Chapter 2

Personal Journeys of Resilience

Stories of Fearful Beginnings

In the journey of entrepreneurship, many start with a heart full of ambition but also a mind clouded by fear. The stories of those who have navigated this treacherous terrain often reveal a common thread: a fearful beginning that transformed into a powerful narrative of success. Take, for instance, the story of a young woman who dreamed of launching her own bakery.

Despite her passion for baking, she was paralysed by the fear of failure. The thought of financial instability and disappointing her loved ones loomed large. Yet, it was in facing her fears that she found the courage to take the first step, testing her recipes at local markets and gathering feedback. Each small victory chipped away at her anxiety, ultimately paving the way for her.

Another inspiring tale comes from a former corporate employee who decided to leave the security of a steady paycheck to pursue his dream of creating an app. The fear of the unknown was overwhelming; he wrestled with self-doubt and the potential for financial ruin. However, he took the leap after countless nights spent researching and developing his idea. What began as a fearful venture soon turned into a relentless pursuit of innovation. Each setback became a lesson, and each lesson fueled his determination. Today, his app is a staple in the industry, a testament to how embracing fear can lead to remarkable outcomes.

Then there is the story of a man who had always been fascinated by fashion but felt trapped in a career that did not align with his passion. The fear of judgment from peers and family kept him in his comfort zone for years. One day, however, he decided enough was enough. He began sketching designs in his spare time, pouring his heart into every fabric and stitch. The initial fear of rejection was daunting, but as he shared his creations on social media, he found a supportive community that encouraged him. Gradually, this once timid individual emerged as a successful designer, proving that the path from fear to fulfillment is often paved with creativity and resilience.

In the world of entrepreneurship, the stakes can feel high, and fear can be a formidable adversary. Yet, the story of a tech startup founder illustrates how fear can be transformed into a driving force. Faced with the looming threat of competition and the pressure to succeed, she began by surrounding herself with mentors who had faced similar challenges. Their experiences served as a beacon of hope, illuminating her path and encouraging her to push through the anxiety. By embracing her fear and seeking support, she not only launched her company but also built a network of like-minded individuals who uplifted one another in times of doubt.

Finally, we cannot overlook the journey of those who turn their fear of failure into a catalyst for growth. A social entrepreneur, driven by a desire to address societal issues, initially struggled with the enormity of her vision. The fear of inadequacy loomed large, threatening to overshadow her aspirations. However, she learned to reframe her fear as a necessary component of growth. By starting small, testing her ideas in the community, and learning from feedback, she gradually expanded her reach. Her story is a powerful reminder that even the most fearful beginnings can lead to profound change, not only for oneself but for the world at large. Each of these stories serves as a beacon of inspiration, encouraging us all to embrace our fears and transform them into action.

Turning Setbacks into Comebacks

Every entrepreneur faces setbacks, moments that challenge their resolve and make them question their path. However, these obstacles can become the very catalysts for growth and transformation. The journey of entrepreneurship is rarely a straight line; it is often marked by twists and turns that test our grit. When we encounter failures, it is easy to succumb to fear and doubt. Yet, those who rise to the occasion and view setbacks as opportunities for learning and reinvention often emerge stronger and more focused on their goals.

Consider the story of a young entrepreneur who launched a tech startup with high hopes. After an initial surge of excitement and early adoption, the company faced a significant setback when a competitor released a superior product. This moment could have spelt disaster, but instead of giving in to despair, the entrepreneur gathered feedback, engaged with customers, and identified the core issues that needed addressing. By turning to the very people who had once supported her, she transformed her setbacks into actionable insights, ultimately leading to a revamped product that resonated even more with her audience.

This process of reframing setbacks is a powerful tool in the entrepreneur's toolkit. It requires a shift in mindset, from viewing failure as a definitive endpoint to seeing it as a stepping stone toward success. The most successful entrepreneurs often share that their greatest lessons came from their lowest points. They learned to embrace discomfort and uncertainty, recognising that each setback carried within it the seeds of a comeback. This perspective encourages resilience, fostering a culture of innovation where fear of failure is replaced by curiosity and determination.

Moreover, turning setbacks into comebacks is not just about individual perseverance; it often involves building a supportive network. Surrounding oneself with mentors, peers, and like-minded individuals can provide the encouragement and perspective needed during tough times. The collective wisdom of a community can illuminate paths that may not have been visible in isolation. When setbacks occur, reaching out for support can transform moments of doubt into opportunities for collaboration and shared growth, propelling everyone forward.

Ultimately, the journey of turning setbacks into comebacks is a testament to the indomitable spirit of entrepreneurship. Each challenge faced is an invitation to dig deeper, re-innovate. As you navigate the tumultuous waters of your entrepreneurial journey, remember that fear and failure are not the end but rather integral parts of the process. Embrace them, learn from them, and let them guide you toward your next great achievement. By transforming anxiety into action, you can create a powerful narrative of resilience that inspires not only yourself but also those around you.

Lessons Learned from Failure

Failure is often viewed as a daunting threat, lurking in the shadows of entrepreneurial ambition. Yet, it is within the depths of failure that the seeds of resilience and innovation are sown. Each setback carries with it invaluable lessons that can transform our approach to business and life. Embracing failure as a teacher rather than a deterrent empowers us to confront our fears and emerge stronger. The stories of successful entrepreneurs reveal that their greatest growth often stemmed from their most significant failures, illustrating that the path to achievement is rarely linear.

When we encounter failure, the instinct is often to retreat, to hide from the world and the discomfort of disappointment. However, it is precisely in these moments of vulnerability that we discover our true selves. Many entrepreneurs, after facing major setbacks, found that introspection led them to re-evaluate their goals and values. This self-awareness became the foundation for their next venture, fueling a passion that was previously dormant. By inviting failure into our narrative, we learn to embrace our imperfections and develop a more profound understanding of what drives us.

The fear of failure can be paralysing, but the stories of those who have faced it head-on serve as beacons of hope. Take, for example, the tale of an entrepreneur who launched a promising startup only to see it crumble within a year. Instead of succumbing to despair, they chose to analyse what went wrong. This critical evaluation led to insights about market needs, customer engagement, and the importance of adaptability. Armed with this newfound knowledge, they embarked on a new venture that not only succeeded but thrived, illustrating that failure is not the end; it is merely a stepping stone toward greatness.

Moreover, failure cultivates resilience, an essential trait for any entrepreneur. Each stumble provides an opportunity to rise again, to strategies, and to build a more robust foundation for future endeavours. Many successful entrepreneurs have shared how their experiences with failure taught them to embrace uncertainty and navigate challenges with grace. By shifting our mindset to view obstacles as opportunities for growth, we develop a fearless attitude that propels us forward, allowing us to tackle even the most daunting projects with confidence.

In conclusion, the lessons learned from failure are transformative, shaping not only our professional journeys but also our personal lives. By reframing our relationship with failure, we can dismantle the fear that holds us back and instead cultivate a spirit of courage and tenacity. The path of entrepreneurship is fraught with risks, but within each failure lies the potential for profound learning and growth. As we share these stories of resilience, let us remember that it is not the fall that defines us, but how we rise and what we learn along the way.

Chapter 3

The Mindset Shift

Cultivating a Growth Mindset

Cultivating a growth mindset is essential for anyone aiming to conquer the fears that often accompany entrepreneurship. At its core, a growth mindset is the belief that abilities and intelligence can be developed through dedication and hard work. This perspective fosters resilience and a love for learning, which are vital for navigating the unpredictable journey of entrepreneurship. Embracing this mindset allows you to view challenges not as insurmountable obstacles but as opportunities for growth and learning.

When you encounter setbacks, your response can define your path forward. Instead of succumbing to feelings of inadequacy or fear of failure, a growth mindset encourages you to analyse what went wrong and how you can improve. For instance, many successful entrepreneurs have faced rejection and failure. They recognised these experiences as stepping stones rather than roadblocks. By reframing your failures as valuable lessons, you create a foundation for future success and develop the resilience needed to push through tough times.

Surrounding yourself with a community that values growth can significantly impact your own mindset. Engage with like-minded individuals who share their experiences, insights, and encouragement. By doing so, you'll be part of a supportive network that celebrates effort, persistence, and learning from mistakes. This communal approach not only reinforces your belief in growth but also provides you with inspiration and motivation to challenge yourself continuously. Remember, entrepreneurship is not a solitary endeavour; it's a journey best taken with others who are committed to personal and collective growth.

Practising self-reflection is another crucial aspect of cultivating a growth mindset. Take time to evaluate your thoughts and behaviours regularly. Ask yourself what skills you want to develop and what fears might be holding you back. Journaling can be a powerful tool in this process, allowing you to articulate your thoughts and track your progress. Reflecting your journey helps you recognise patterns, celebrate small victories, and identify areas for improvement. By engaging in this practice, you can transform anxiety into actionable steps that propel you forward.

Finally, embracing a growth mindset requires patience and persistence. Change does not happen overnight, and the road to overcoming fear is often. Celebrate your progress, no matter how small, and maintain a long-term vision for your goals. With each step forward, you will become more comfortable with uncertainty and more adept at navigating the challenges of entrepreneurship. Ultimately, cultivating a growth mindset empowers you to transform fear into action, enabling you to pursue your dreams with confidence and courage.

The Role of Self-Compassion

Self-compassion is a transformative force that can redefine the entrepreneurial journey. As entrepreneurs, we often grapple with self-doubt, fear of failure, and the relentless pursuit of perfection. This can lead to a cycle of anxiety that stifles creativity and hinders progress. However, by embracing self-compassion, we can shift our perspective and cultivate a more nurturing relationship with ourselves. This not only allows us to acknowledge our imperfections but also empowers us to view failures as opportunities for growth rather than as reflection of our worth.

When we practice self-compassion, we learn to treat ourselves with the same kindness and understanding that we would offer to a friend. This shift is vital in entrepreneurship, where the stakes can feel incredibly high. Each setback can trigger harsh self-criticism, but by fostering self-compassion, we begin to recognise that everyone faces challenges. We are not alone in our struggles, and understanding this can alleviate some of the pressures we place on ourselves. Such a realisation can be liberating, allowing us to approach our ventures with renewed energy and optimism.

Self-compassion also plays a crucial role in enhancing resilience. Facing the inevitable ups and downs of entrepreneurship requires a strong foundation of emotional strength. When we are kind to ourselves in moments of despair, we build the capacity to bounce back from setbacks.

Instead of becoming paralysed by fear, we learn to embrace challenges as integral parts of our journey. This resilience is essential not only for personal growth but also for the sustainability of our businesses. An entrepreneur who practices self-compassion is better equipped to navigate the turbulent waters of uncertainty with grace and determination.

Moreover, self-compassion fosters a growth mindset, encouraging us to view our skills and abilities as something that can be developed over time. This perspective is particularly important in entrepreneurship, where learning and adaptation are key to success. By permitting ourselves to make mistakes without severe self-criticism, we foster an environment that encourages innovation. This approach enables individuals to take calculated risks, pursue novel ideas, and adapt effectively when changes are required. This adaptability is what separates successful entrepreneurs from those who remain stagnant in the face of fear.

Ultimately, self-compassion is not just a personal practice; it is a powerful tool that can enhance our entrepreneurial journey. By cultivating a compassionate mindset, we not only improve our own well-being but also inspire those around us. By sharing experiences of overcoming fear and embracing vulnerability, we foster a supportive community that enables individuals to grow. Practising self-compassion serves as a catalyst for collective development, encouraging everyone to confront their fears and translate them into concrete actions that drive success.

Visualisation Techniques for Success

Visualisation techniques serve as powerful tools for entrepreneurs looking to transform their dreams into reality. At its core, visualisation is the practice of creating vivid mental images of desired outcomes. This technique allows individuals to see their goals clearly, facilitating a deeper connection to the steps required to achieve them. For aspiring entrepreneurs, visualising success can ignite the motivation needed to conquer fears and embrace the challenges that lie ahead. Consistent engagement in this practice enables individuals to develop a clear roadmap that effectively directs their progress toward both personal and professional goals.

One effective visualisation technique involves creating a vision board. This tangible representation of goals and aspirations serves as a daily reminder of what one is working toward. Entrepreneurs can gather images, quotes, and symbols that resonate with their dreams and arrange them on a board. Placing this board in a visible area allows for constant inspiration and serves to reinforce the belief in their potential. Every glance at the vision board reminds them not only of their goals but also of the emotions associated with achieving them, transforming abstract dreams into concrete targets.

Another powerful visualisation method is guided imagery. This technique invites individuals to engage in deep relaxation and mental imagery, allowing them to experience their goals in a sensory-rich context. By closing their eyes and imagining themselves successfully navigating challenges, pitching ideas, or celebrating milestones, entrepreneurs can create a mental rehearsal that prepares them for real-life scenarios. This practice reduces anxiety by familiarising the mind with success, enabling individuals to approach situations with a sense of calm and readiness.

Incorporating affirmations into visualisation can further enhance its effectiveness. Positive affirmations, when combined with visual imagery, create a potent synergy that reinforces self-belief. Entrepreneurs can repeat empowering phrases while visualising their success, effectively programming their subconscious mind to align with their aspirations. This repeated affirmations of one's capabilities helps to dismantle the barriers of fear and self-doubt, paving the way for courageous action. The more one internalises these messages, the more resilient they become in the face of adversity.

Ultimately, visualisation techniques empower entrepreneurs to take ownership of their journeys. By consciously envisioning their success, they cultivate an inner strength that propels them forward, even when faced with uncertainty. These techniques not only enhance focus and clarity but also inspire a fearless mindset that transforms anxiety into action. As individuals embrace the art of visualisation, they unlock their potential, paving the way for personal success stories that resonate beyond their own experiences, inspiring others to follow suit.

Chapter 4

Building a Supportive Network

The Importance of Mentorship

Mentorship is a powerful catalyst in the journey of entrepreneurship. It offers not just guidance but also a sense of reassurance that you are not alone in your struggles. When faced with fear and uncertainty, having an experienced mentor can illuminate the path ahead. They provide insight gained from their own experiences, helping you to navigate the challenges that accompany launching and running a business. This relationship fosters a learning environment where questions can be asked, mistakes can be discussed, and fears can be confronted. Through mentorship, you gain not only knowledge but also a renewed sense of confidence.

The benefits of mentorship extend beyond just practical advice; they also encompass emotional support. Entrepreneurs often grapple with self-doubt and anxiety. A mentor, having faced similar hurdles, can share stories of their own fears and failures, making it clear that setbacks are a natural part of the entrepreneurial journey. This shared experience can be immensely comforting, reminding you that fear does not indicate weakness but rather a sign that you are pushing your boundaries. Learning how others turn fears into strengths can help you move forward.

Moreover, mentorship provides networking opportunities that can prove invaluable. A mentor often has a wealth of connections that can open doors for you, facilitating introductions to potential partners, investors, or clients. These relationships can be crucial, especially in times of uncertainty. Knowing that someone believes in your vision and is willing to advocate for you can help mitigate the fear of rejection or failure. This network can serve as a safety net, allowing you to take calculated risks that might have seemed daunting if you were navigating the landscape alone.

Additionally, mentorship encourages accountability. When you have someone to report your progress to, your goals become more tangible. This accountability can help you push through the fear that often accompanies stepping out of your comfort zone. Your mentor can inspire you to set ambitious targets and hold you accountable for reaching them. This external pressure can often be the nudge you need to take that leap of faith, transforming anxiety into tangible action and progress.

Ultimately, the relationship between a mentor and a mentee is one of mutual growth and development. As you progress on your entrepreneurial journey, you may find that you have valuable lessons to share with others. This cycle of mentorship not only strengthens your own resolve but also empowers the next generation of entrepreneurs. By embracing mentorship, you tap into a rich resource that can help you not only overcome your fears but also transform them into stepping stones toward your success.

Finding Your Tribe: Networking for Success

Finding your tribe is one of the most empowering steps you can take on your entrepreneurial journey. As you navigate the often turbulent waters of starting and growing a business, the support and guidance of like-minded individuals can make all the difference. These connections not only help you overcome fear but also inspire you to push through challenges. When you surround yourself with people who share your vision, goals, and struggles, you create a community that fuels your passion and determination.

Networking is not just about exchanging business cards or making contacts; it's about building meaningful relationships. Seek out individuals who resonate with your story, those who understand the fears and doubts that come with entrepreneurship. Attend local meetups, join online forums, and participate in workshops, all of which can serve as platforms for your tribe. Each encounter is an opportunity to share experiences, gain insights, and foster connections that can lead to collaborations and partnerships that elevate your business.

In your quest for connection, remember that vulnerability is a strength. Sharing your fears and challenges with others can forge deeper bonds and create a safe space for open dialogue. When you allow yourself to be authentic, you not only attract the right people into your life but also inspire others to do the same. Every entrepreneur has faced obstacles, and by sharing your personal stories, you can create a powerful narrative that resonates with those around you, fostering an environment of support and encouragement.

Additionally, consider leveraging social media and online platforms to expand your network beyond geographical limitations. Many entrepreneurs have found success through virtual communities where they can connect, share ideas, and collaborate without the constraints of location. Engage actively in discussions, provide value through your insights, and don't hesitate to reach out to those who inspire you. The digital world thrives on mutual support, and a single connection can create significant opportunities.

Ultimately, a tribe is about creating a foundation of support that empowers you to confront and conquer your fears. As you build these relationships, remember that networking is a two-way street. Be willing to offer help, share resources, and celebrate the successes of others. When you cultivate a community rooted in mutual support and encouragement, you not only elevate your entrepreneurial journey but also contribute to a culture of fearless action, paving the way for collective success.

Sharing Stories to Inspire

In the realm of entrepreneurship, fear often looms large, casting shadows over dreams and aspirations. Yet, within this darkness, stories of triumph shine brightly, illuminating the path for others. Sharing stories of personal struggles and victories not only serves as a source of inspiration but also fosters a sense of community among those navigating similar challenges. Each narrative holds the potential to resonate deeply, reminding us that fear is a universal experience, one that can be transformed into a catalyst for growth and success.

Consider the example of an entrepreneur who once stood paralysed by self-doubt, questioning every decision and fearing the judgment of others. Through perseverance, this individual learned to embrace vulnerability, sharing their journey with others who felt the same weight of uncertainty. By articulating their fears and the steps taken to overcome them, they offered a beacon of hope, encouraging fellow entrepreneurs to confront their anxieties head-on. This act of sharing not only empowered the narrator but also inspired others to take bold steps toward their own aspirations.

In another inspiring account, a business owner faced numerous rejections while seeking investors for a groundbreaking idea. Each rejection felt like a personal failure, chipping away at their confidence. However, by recounting this experience to a group of aspiring entrepreneurs, they found solidarity in shared struggles. This story highlighted the importance of resilience and the understanding that every setback is merely a stepping stone on the path to success. The lesson learned was clear: vulnerability can transform fear into a powerful narrative that encourages others to persist despite the odds.

Stories also have the power to shift perspectives, revealing that fear does not have to dictate the terms of our journey. A successful entrepreneur once shared how they learned to view fear as a companion rather than an enemy. By embracing fear as a natural part of the process, they cultivated a mindset that allowed them to take calculated risks, ultimately leading to innovation and growth. This perspective resonated with many, demonstrating that sharing such insights can inspire a collective shift in how we perceive our fears.

Ultimately, sharing stories is a powerful tool in the entrepreneurial toolkit. It creates a tapestry of experiences that bind individuals together, fostering a culture of support and encouragement. By opening up about fears and vulnerabilities, entrepreneurs can create a safe space for dialogue, where others feel empowered to share their own stories. In doing so, we not only inspire action but also cultivate a community that celebrates resilience, reminding us all that we are not alone in our struggles and that fear can be transformed into an engine for success.

Chapter 5

Practical Strategies for Action

Setting Achievable Goals

Setting achievable goals is the cornerstone of transforming anxiety into action and fostering a fearless entrepreneurial spirit. Achievable goals provide a roadmap for navigating the often turbulent waters of entrepreneurship. When we break down our larger aspirations into smaller, manageable steps, we create a sense of direction and purpose. This structured approach not only alleviates the overwhelming feelings that can accompany ambitious dreams but also instils a sense of accomplishment as we progress. Each small victory paves the way for greater confidence and resilience, reinforcing our commitment to overcoming fear.

To begin setting achievable goals, it is essential to embrace the concept of specificity. Vague aspirations can lead to confusion and frustration, while clearly defined objectives act as a guiding star. Rather than stating, "I want to be successful," a more specific goal could be, "I will launch my online business within six months and achieve my target by the end of the third month." Providing this level of detail defines the objective clearly and establishes a timeline, which helps in developing actionable steps toward achieving it. When you know exactly what you're working towards, it becomes easier to muster the courage needed to take that leap.

Breaking larger goals into smaller milestones can significantly reduce feelings of intimidation and anxiety. Each milestone serves as a checkpoint along your journey, allowing you to celebrate progress and adjust your strategies as needed. For example, if your goal is to build a successful consultancy, focus on branding, networking in your field, and landing your first clients. By concentrating on these smaller tasks, you can maintain momentum and stay motivated, even when the path ahead appears daunting. Remember, every successful entrepreneur has faced uncertainty; it is the small, consistent actions that ultimately lead to monumental achievements.

Accountability plays a crucial role in successfully setting and achieving goals. Sharing your aspirations with trusted friends, mentors, or fellow entrepreneurs can create a network of support that encourages you to stay committed to your objectives. When others are aware of your goals, they can help hold you accountable, providing motivation and constructive feedback along the way. Surrounding yourself with a community of like-minded individuals can also inspire you to push through fear and self-doubt, as you witness their own journeys of overcoming obstacles. The collective energy of ambition can ignite your own passion and drive.

Lastly, it is vital to remain adaptable in the face of challenges. The entrepreneurial journey is rarely a straight path; it is filled with unexpected twists and turns. When setbacks occur, rather than viewing them as failures, consider them as valuable learning experiences that can inform future strategies. Adjusting your goals to accommodate new insights and circumstances does not signify weakness; it illustrates resilience and a commitment to growth. By maintaining a flexible mindset, you empower yourself to navigate uncertainty with courage, transforming anxiety into a powerful catalyst for action. Embrace the journey, celebrate your milestones, and continue to set achievable goals that propel you forward in your entrepreneurial adventure.

Overcoming Procrastination

Procrastination can feel like an unshakable burden, particularly for entrepreneurs who are often navigating the treacherous waters of uncertainty and self-doubt. It sneaks into our lives, disguised as busy work or the need for "just one more perfect revision." The truth is, every moment spent delaying action is a moment lost to fear. The journey to overcoming procrastination begins with the realisation that the fear of failure often paralyses us, but it doesn't have to define our paths. Embracing the discomfort of taking action, even when we feel unprepared, can ignite a transformation that propels us forward.

One of the most powerful tools in overcoming procrastination is reframing our mindset around failure. Rather than viewing it as a disaster, we can see it as a valuable lesson. Each misstep carries insights that can shape our future decisions. Successful entrepreneurs often share stories of their own failures, revealing that these experiences were pivotal in building their resilience and fortitude. By adopting this perspective, we transform procrastination from a fear of the unknown into an opportunity for growth. It's about understanding that every action we take, regardless of the outcome, moves us closer to our ultimate goals.

Setting clear and achievable goals is another vital strategy to combat procrastination. When we break down our larger ambitions into smaller, manageable tasks, we create a roadmap that guides us through the fog of indecision. Celebrating these small victories not only builds momentum but also reinforces our self-belief. Each completed task serves as a stepping stone, leading us to the next phase of our journey. By focusing on progress rather than perfection, we can dismantle the overwhelming nature of our aspirations and ignite a sense of accomplishment that fuels our motivation.

Establishing a routine can also play a crucial role in overcoming procrastination. Consistency breeds discipline, and when we create a structured environment for our work, we reduce the likelihood of distractions and delays. This could mean setting specific hours dedicated solely to our entrepreneurial pursuits or creating a workspace that inspires creativity and focus. By building habits that support our goals, we create a fertile ground for productivity. The more we honour our commitments to ourselves, the more empowered we become in our entrepreneurial journeys.

Finally, finding a support system can be incredibly beneficial in overcoming procrastination. Surrounding ourselves with like-minded individuals who share our aspirations can provide the encouragement we need to push through moments of doubt. Whether through networking events, online communities, or mentorship programs, connecting with others can help us stay accountable and inspired. Sharing our struggles and triumphs creates a collective energy that fosters resilience. By leaning on each other, we not only combat procrastination but also create a network of support that reinforces our courage to take bold action.

Creating a Fear-Action Plan

Creating a Fear-Action Plan involves recognising that fear is a natural part of the entrepreneurial journey. Every successful entrepreneur has faced moments of doubt and anxiety. What sets them apart is their ability to confront these feelings head-on and transform them into powerful motivators. A Fear-Action Plan is not merely a strategy; it is a commitment to harness the energy of fear and channel it into productive action. By acknowledging fear as a companion rather than an enemy, entrepreneurs can pave the way to their personal and professional growth.

The first step in crafting your Fear-Action Plan is to identify the specific fears that hold you back. Take a moment to reflect on your aspirations and the obstacles that seem insurmountable. Are you afraid of failure, rejection, or the unknown? Write these fears down, as they will serve as the foundation for your plan. This act of acknowledgement is liberating; it transforms intangible worries into concrete challenges that can be addressed. Remember, the act of writing creates clarity, and clarity is the first step toward overcoming the barriers that fear erects.

Once you have identified your fears, the next step is to break them down into manageable components. Instead of viewing fear as a monolith, dissect it into smaller, actionable pieces. For example, if the fear of failure looms large, consider the smaller fears that contribute to it, such as the fear of not meeting expectations or the fear of components can be tackled individually. By creating specific, actionable steps to address each fear, you empower yourself to take control of the narrative. This process not only demystifies your fears but also cultivates resilience and confidence.

As you implement your Fear-Action Plan, it is essential to set measurable goals. Establish clear milestones that allow you to track your progress. Celebrate small victories along the way, whether it's making that difficult phone call presenting your ideas, or launching a new project. Each achievement, no matter how small, reinforces your ability to face fear and emerge stronger. This positive reinforcement creates a feedback loop that builds self-esteem, reminding you that fear does not define you; your actions do.

Finally, share your journey with others. Surround yourself with a supportive community of like-minded individuals who are also navigating their fears. Sharing your experiences fosters connection and provides a platform for mutual encouragement. As you open up about your struggles and triumphs, you inspire others to embark on their own Fear-Action Plan. Remember, the most impactful stories of personal success often arise from the depths of fear. By transforming your anxiety into action, you not only elevate your own journey but also empower others to embrace their fears and pursue their dreams with unwavering courage.

Chapter 6

Celebrating Small Wins

Recognising Progress

Recognising progress is a vital aspect of any entrepreneurial journey, especially for those grappling with fear and anxiety. As you embark on this path, it can often feel overwhelming. However, acknowledging your small victories can illuminate the path ahead, transforming your anxiety into actionable steps. Each milestone, no matter how minor it may seem, is a testament to your courage and resilience. By taking a moment to reflect on these achievements, you can build momentum and foster a mindset that embraces growth rather than fear.

Consider the story of Sarah, a budding entrepreneur who once felt paralysed by self-doubt. She started her journey by setting attainable goals, such as attending networking events or reaching out to potential mentors. At first, these steps felt daunting, but with each event she attended, she gained confidence and valuable insights. Recognising her progress was crucial; it allowed her to see that each conversation and connection was a building block toward her ultimate vision. By celebrating these small wins, Sarah transformed her anxiety into a source of motivation, propelling her forward in her entrepreneurial endeavours.

Tracking progress can take many forms, from journaling experiences to setting up visual reminders of your achievements. The act of documenting your journey serves not only as a record of where you've been but also as a source of inspiration during challenging times. When you look back at what you have accomplished, you create a tangible reminder that progress is possible. Even on the days when fear looms large, these reflections can serve as a beacon of hope and encouragement, reminding you of your strength and capability to overcome obstacles.

Moreover, recognising progress is not just about celebrating successes; it also involves acknowledging the lessons learned from failures. Each setback is an opportunity to grow, a chance to re-evaluate your approach and strengthen your resolve. Embracing this perspective allows you to see fear not as a barrier but as a teacher. For example, James encountered several rejections when presenting his business ideas. He subsequently worked on his presentation skills and focused on understanding his audience. By viewing these experiences as part of his development, he changed his approach from seeing setbacks as failures to focusing on ongoing improvement.

Ultimately, the journey of entrepreneurship is not a straight path but a winding road with ups and downs. By recognising progress, you empower yourself to move beyond fear and into action. Remember, every step you take, no matter how small, is a victory worth acknowledging.

Embrace your growth and let it drive your passion. As you appreciate your progress, fear fades, empowering you to confidently pursue your entrepreneurial journey.

The Power of Gratitude

Gratitude is a transformative force that can significantly alter our mindsets, especially for entrepreneurs navigating the often turbulent waters of business ownership. In the face of fear and uncertainty, expressing gratitude can shift our focus from what we lack to what we already possess. This simple yet profound practice allows us to recognise the abundance in our lives, fostering resilience and creativity. When we actively acknowledge the support of our networks, the lessons learned from failures, and the progress we have made, we cultivate a sense of empowerment that propels us forward.

Many successful entrepreneurs have harnessed the power of gratitude to overcome their fears and propel their businesses to new heights. Take the story of a young entrepreneur who faced numerous rejections before launching her startup. Rather than dwelling on the setbacks, she began a daily gratitude journal, listing three things she was thankful for each morning. This practice shifted her perspective, enabling her to see rejections as stepping stones rather than roadblocks. As she celebrated small wins and appreciated the lessons learned along the way, her confident grew, and so did her business.

Gratitude also fosters stronger connections with others, which is vital in entrepreneurship. Building a network of supporters can be daunting, especially when fear creeps in. However, when we express genuine appreciation for others, whether it's a mentor, a colleague, or a customer, we create an environment of trust and collaboration. This atmosphere not only encourages open communication but also inspires others to reciprocate that kindness. In turn, these relationships can become invaluable sources of support, advice, and inspiration, helping us navigate our entrepreneurial journey with greater assurance.

The impact of gratitude extends beyond personal well-being; it can also enhance our decision-making process. When we approach challenges with a grateful mindset, we are more likely to remain calm and focused, allowing us to make thoughtful choices instead of reactive ones. This clarity can be especially beneficial when facing fears that threaten to paralyse us. By acknowledging the positive aspects of our situations, we create mental space for innovative solutions to emerge, transforming fear into actionable strategies that lead to growth and success.

Ultimately, embracing gratitude is not just a feel-good exercise; it is a powerful tool for overcoming fear and achieving entrepreneurial success. By incorporating gratitude into our daily routines, we can cultivate a mindset that empowers us to face challenges head-on. As we acknowledge our strengths and the support around us, we build an unshakeable foundation that allows us to take bold actions, pursue our dreams, and transform our anxieties into opportunities. In this journey, gratitude is not merely a reaction to our circumstances but a proactive choice that fuels our fearless entrepreneurial spirit.

Using Milestones to Fuel Motivation

Milestones serve as powerful markers along the entrepreneurial journey, transforming abstract goals into tangible achievements that can fuel motivation. Each milestone reached is not just a destination but a celebration of progress, a reminder of how far one has come despite the fears that may have threatened to hold them back. By setting these milestones, entrepreneurs can break their larger, often daunting goals into manageable steps, allowing them to experience a sense of accomplishment at various stages along the way. This approach not only reinforces their commitment but also cultivates a mindset geared toward resilience and triumph.

When encountering anxiety and fear, some entrepreneurs may experience uncertainty about their abilities and decisions. Recognising and celebrating milestones can help reinforce confidence by highlighting progress. Each time a milestone is achieved and acknowledged, it shifts attention from outstanding tasks to completed goals, which can contribute to sustained motivation throughout the process.

Moreover, milestones can act as anchors during turbulent times. Entrepreneurship is ups and downs, often accompanied by self-doubt and uncertainty. By looking back at the milestones achieved, individuals can draw strength from their past successes, reminding themselves that they have navigated challenges before and can do so again. This fosters a sense of continuity and purpose, encouraging entrepreneurs to push through difficult periods with the knowledge that they are capable of achieving great things.

The journey of entrepreneurship is often shared, and celebrating milestones with a community can amplify motivation even further. Whether it's through sharing achievements with friends, family, or fellow entrepreneurs, the collective acknowledgement can provide a sense of belonging and encouragement. When others celebrate your achievements, it affirms your efforts and reminds you that your journey is shared. This collective recognition turns personal wins into group motivation.

Ultimately, using milestones to fuel motivation is about more than just reaching goals; it's about cultivating a mindset rooted in growth and resilience. Each milestone serves as a reminder that fear can be transformed into action and that every step taken, no matter how small, is a step toward success. By embracing the process of setting and celebrating milestones, entrepreneurs can not only conquer their fears but also inspire others to embark on their own journeys with courage and conviction. In this way, milestones become not just markers of progress, but powerful catalysts for ongoing motivation and personal growth in the entrepreneurial landscape.

Chapter 7

Staying Fearless in the Face of Adversity

Resilience in Tough Times

Resilience in tough times is more than just a buzzword; it is a crucial mindset that separates successful entrepreneurs from those who falter. When faced with challenges, the ability to bounce back, adapt, and grow is what transforms a fearful entrepreneur into a fearless one. The journey of entrepreneurship is often fraught with uncertainty, unexpected setbacks. However, within these hardships lies the opportunity for personal growth and the development of a resilient spirit that can weather any storm.

Consider the story of Anisha, a budding entrepreneur who launched her small bakery in a competitive market. Just as she began to gain traction, a sudden economic downturn forced many of her potential customers to cut back on non-essential spending. Rather than succumbing to despair, Anisha embraced the challenge. She pivoted her business model to include online orders and local delivery, leveraging social media to reach a broader audience. Through her resilience, she not only survived the tough times but emerged stronger, learning valuable lessons in adaptability and innovation.

Resilience is often cultivated through a combination of self-awareness and a strong support system. Entrepreneurs who actively seek feedback and surround themselves with mentors or like-minded individuals are better equipped to navigate their fears and insecurities, they can confront them head-on rather than allowing them to dictate their actions. This proactive approach transforms setbacks into stepping stones, reinforcing the belief that challenges are merely opportunities for growth.

Moreover, maintaining a positive mindset is essential in fostering resilience. Entrepreneurs who practice gratitude, even in the face of adversity, can shift their perspective from one of scarcity to one of abundance. This shift allows them to see beyond immediate problems and focus on long-term goals. By celebrating small victories and learning from failures, they build a mental toolkit that empowers them to tackle future challenges with confidence and determination.

Ultimately, resilience in tough times is about embracing the journey, no matter how rocky it may be. Each setback is a lesson in disguise, offering insights that can lead to greater success. By sharing stories of overcoming fear and adversity, we inspire others to recognise their own strength in the face of challenges. As we navigate the unpredictable waters of entrepreneurship, let us remember that it is our resilience that will light the path to our dreams, turning anxiety into action and fear into fearless determination.

Embracing Change and Uncertainty

Embracing change and uncertainty is a vital skill for anyone on the entrepreneurial journey. In the world of business, where the only constant is change, the ability to adapt and thrive can mean the difference between success and stagnation. Rather than viewing uncertainty as a threat, consider it an opportunity for growth and innovation. Each shift in the landscape presents a chance to pivot, to explore new avenues, and to redefine your vision. The most successful entrepreneurs are those who approach change with a sense of curiosity rather than fear, understanding that each challenge is a stepping stone toward their ultimate goals.

Uncertainty often causes anxiety, but this can be a motivator. Many entrepreneurs channel fear into action, building resilience by learning from past experiences. Stepping outside your comfort zone in uncertain times helps you discover your potential, as breakthroughs often emerge from discomfort and unpredictability.

Moreover, cultivating a mindset that welcomes change fosters a culture of innovation. When you embrace uncertainty, you empower yourself to experiment, take calculated risks, and learn from failures. Fear of mistakes can be paralysing, but seeing failure as part of the process puts you in a better position to succeed.

Each setback can be a teacher, equipping you with valuable insights that can inform your future decisions. By sharing your own experiences and the lessons learned along the way, you can inspire others to view their challenges through a lens of possibility.

Community support plays a crucial role in navigating change and uncertainty. Surrounding yourself with like-minded individuals who share similar aspirations can create a safe space for open dialogue about fears and challenges. These connections can provide invaluable encouragement and diverse perspectives that enrich your understanding of the entrepreneurial landscape. Engaging with mentors, peers, and other entrepreneurs can help you gain confidence as you confront the unknown, reminding you that you are not alone in your journey.

Ultimately, embracing change and uncertainty is about cultivating a fearless spirit. Each time you confront your fears, you build a foundation of courage and resilience that propels you forward. The entrepreneurial path is rarely a straight line, but those who learn to dance with uncertainty emerge stronger and more adaptable. As you reflect on your own journey, consider how embracing change has shaped your path. By transforming anxiety into action, you not only pave the way for personal success but also inspire others to embrace their fears and chase their dreams with unwavering determination.

Maintaining Momentum

Maintaining momentum in the entrepreneurial journey is crucial, especially when faced with the inevitable challenges and fears that arise. It is easy to feel exhilarated at the beginning of a venture, fueled by dreams and the thrill of possibility. However, as obstacles emerge, that initial spark can dim, leading to hesitation and doubt. To sustain momentum, it is essential to cultivate a mindset that embraces resilience and adaptability. By recognising that setbacks are not failures but rather opportunities for growth, entrepreneurs can maintain their drive and continue moving forward with confidence.

Celebrating small wins is key for keeping momentum. Each achievement, however minor, adds to overall progress and builds confidence. Recognising these successes can motivate you to keep moving forward by creating a positive cycle of action.

Accountability also plays a significant role in sustaining momentum. Sharing goals with trusted friends, mentors, or fellow entrepreneurs can create a support system that fosters commitment. By articulating one's aspirations and inviting others to check in periodically, individuals are more likely to stay focused and driven. This social aspect of accountability can transform isolation into a shared journey, where encouragement and constructive feedback propel progress. Moreover, engaging with like-minded individuals can provide fresh perspectives and innovative ideas, reigniting passion for the work at hand.

Another powerful tool for maintaining momentum is the practice of mindfulness. Taking time to reassess thoughts and feelings can provide clarity and insight, especially when fear begins to creep in. Mindfulness allows entrepreneurs to confront their anxieties head-on, transforming fear into a source of motivation rather than a hindrance. Techniques such as meditation, journaling, or simply taking a moment to breathe can help refocus energy and reinforce the purpose behind one's entrepreneurial pursuits. By cultivating a mindful approach, individuals can navigate their emotional landscape and emerge stronger, ready to tackle the next steps in their journey.

Finally, embracing a growth mindset is essential for maintaining momentum. This perspective encourages individuals to view challenges as opportunities for learning rather than insurmountable barriers. By shifting focus from the fear of failure to the excitement of potential growth, entrepreneurs can navigate their paths with renewed vigour. Each experience, whether successful or not, contributes to a wealth of knowledge that can inform future decisions. As entrepreneurs continue to push through fear and uncertainty, they not only maintain momentum but also pave the way for transformative success that stems from perseverance and unwavering belief in their vision.

Chapter 8

Inspiring Others Through Your Journey

Sharing Your Story for Impact

Sharing your story as an entrepreneur can be a powerful tool for impact, allowing you to connect with others who may be experiencing similar challenges. When you reveal the journey that brought you to where you are today, you invite your audience into your world, showing them that overcoming fear is not just possible but a common experience. Personal success stories are particularly impactful, as they illustrate both the challenges and achievements encountered along the entrepreneurial journey. By sharing your narrative, you inspire others to confront their fears and take action toward their own dreams.

Your story is unique, shaped by your experiences, challenges, and the lessons learned along the way. Embrace the authenticity of your journey, as it has the potential to empower others who may feel isolated in their struggles. When you recount the moments of doubt and fear, you create a sense of relatability. This vulnerability not only fosters connection but also demonstrates that fear is a natural part of the entrepreneurial experience. By showing how you navigated those moments, you provide a roadmap for others who may be feeling lost or overwhelmed.

In sharing your story, focus on the turning points that led to your growth. Highlight specific instances where you faced fear head-on and the strategies you used to overcome it. Perhaps it was a moment of decision that required you to step outside your comfort zone or an inspiring encounter that reignited your passion. These pivotal moments serve as beacons of hope for others who are looking to make changes in their own lives. Your insights can guide and motivate them to grow and pursue their goals.

Moreover, consider the impact of storytelling in building a community. When you share your experiences, you invite dialogue and connection among fellow entrepreneurs. This exchange of stories can create a supportive environment where individuals feel safe to express their fears and aspirations. By fostering a sense of belonging, you empower others to share their own narratives, creating a ripple effect of inspiration and encouragement. Together, you can cultivate a culture that celebrates resilience and the courage to take risks.

Ultimately, sharing your story serves not only as a means of personal reflection, but also as a catalyst for meaningful change. Each story has the potential to inspire action, encouraging others to embrace their fears and pursue their entrepreneurial dreams. As you weave your narrative, remember that your experiences can light the way for someone else navigating their own journey. By being fearless in sharing your truth, you contribute to a collective movement of empowerment, reminding everyone that they are not alone in their struggles and that their stories matter.

Encouraging Others to Take Action

Encouraging others to take action is a powerful way to create a ripple effect of change and motivation. When individuals see someone they admire or relate to stepping outside their comfort zone, it ignites a spark within them. This spark can transform into the courage needed to confront their fears. As we share our personal success stories and the challenges we have overcome, we provide a roadmap for others, illustrating that fear is not a barrier but a stepping stone to success. Each story serves as a testament that taking action, despite the fear, can lead to remarkable outcomes.

To inspire others effectively, it is essential to foster an environment of support and positivity. When people feel safe and encouraged, they are more likely to step out of their comfort zones. This can be achieved through sharing relatable experiences, where vulnerability becomes a strength. By openly discussing our own fears and the actions we took to overcome them, we provide a sense of camaraderie. It is this connection that allows others to see that they are not alone in their struggles and that their aspirations are within reach.

Taking action is often about breaking down the seemingly insurmountable into manageable steps. Encourage those around you to set small, achievable goals that lead to larger accomplishments. This method not only minimises the overwhelming feeling of fear but also builds confidence as each goal is achieved. Celebrating these small victories together not only solidifies their progress but also reinforces a culture of encouragement. When people witness their peers succeeding, they become more willing to take risks and embark on their journeys.

Mentorship is an effective strategy for facilitating action. Through providing guidance and support, mentors assist individuals in addressing their concerns and uncertainties. This professional relationship can serve as a significant source of motivation, enabling mentees to gain valuable perspective and direction.

Mentorship can take many forms, from one-on-one meetings to group workshops. Regardless of the format, the key is to foster open dialogue where fears can be discussed, and strategies for overcoming them can be shared. This collaborative approach not only empowers individuals but also creates a community of fearless entrepreneurs.

Finally, it is vital to remember that taking action is a continuous journey. Encourage others to embrace the inevitable setbacks and challenges they will face along the way. These moments are not failures but opportunities for growth and learning. Remind them that resilience is built through perseverance and that each step taken, no matter how small, is a step towards their dreams. By cultivating this mindset, we can inspire others to not only take action but to embrace the journey of entrepreneurship with open arms, transforming anxiety into a powerful driving force for success.

Building a Legacy of Fearlessness

In the journey of entrepreneurship, fear often emerges as a constant companion, lurking in the shadows of our ambitions. Yet, it is precisely this fear that can be transformed into a powerful force for action. Building a legacy of fearlessness requires a shift in perspective: viewing fear not as an obstacle, but as a catalyst for growth. Every successful entrepreneur has faced moments of uncertainty, yet those who embrace their fear and channel it into productive energy create a lasting impact not only on their ventures but also on the lives of others.

Every success story begins with a decision to confront fear head-on. Consider the entrepreneurs who have turned their struggles into stepping stones. Each of them encountered doubt, whether it was the fear of failure, rejection, or the unknown. By sharing their personal narratives, they inspire others to see that fear is not a sign of weakness but a universal experience. It is through these stories that we learn the importance of resilience and the courage to take that first step, which ultimately lays the foundation for a legacy characterised by fearlessness.

Building this legacy involves cultivating a mindset that embraces challenges as opportunities. Entrepreneurs who have triumphed over their fears often speak of the transformative power of taking risks. They learned to celebrate small wins and view setbacks as valuable lessons. This mindset shift enables them to foster an environment of innovation and creativity, where fear is acknowledged but not allowed to dictate their actions. By modeling this behavior, they inspire their teams and communities to adopt a similar approach, creating a ripple effect of fearlessness that extends far beyond their immediate sphere.

Mentorship and community play crucial roles in this journey. Fearlessness is contagious, and by surrounding ourselves with like-minded individuals, we can amplify our courage. Successful entrepreneurs often emphasise the importance of building networks that offer support and encouragement. These relationships provide the safety net needed to take bold steps and experiment with new ideas. As we share our fears and triumphs, we contribute to a culture that celebrates courage and resilience, laying the groundwork for future entrepreneurs to build their own legacies of fearlessness.

Ultimately, building a legacy of fearlessness is about leaving a mark on the world that inspires others to follow suit. It is a commitment to not only pursue our dreams but also to uplift those around us. By transforming anxiety into action, we create a blueprint for future generations. This legacy transcends individual achievements and becomes a movement, encouraging a collective embrace of fear as a stepping stone to greatness. By doing this, we shape our paths and encourage others to pursue theirs with confidence.

Chapter 9

The Future of Fearless Entrepreneurship

Trends in Entrepreneurial Resilience

In the ever-evolving landscape of entrepreneurship, resilience has emerged as a defining trait among successful entrepreneurs. This resilience is not merely about enduring hardships but transforming challenges into opportunities for growth. The modern entrepreneur navigates a world rife with uncertainty, yet those who embrace resilience not only survive but thrive. This shift from fear to action embodies the spirit of the fearless entrepreneur, who views obstacles as stepping stones rather than roadblocks.

One of the most significant trends in entrepreneurial resilience is the increasing emphasis on mental health and well-being. Entrepreneurs are recognising that their mental fortitude is as crucial as their business acumen. This awareness has led to the rise of resources such as coaching, therapy, and peer support networks specifically tailored for entrepreneurs. By prioritising mental health, individuals can cultivate a more robust foundation, enabling them to face challenges head-on. The stories of entrepreneurs who have turned their mental health struggles into sources of strength serve as powerful reminders that vulnerability can lead to extraordinary resilience.

Another trend is the integration of mindfulness and emotional intelligence into entrepreneurial practices. Entrepreneurs are learning to manage their emotions and stress levels through mindfulness techniques, such as meditation and deep breathing exercises. These practices allow them to remain centred and focused, even in the face of adversity. By developing emotional intelligence, entrepreneurs can better navigate interpersonal relationships, fostering collaboration and support within their teams. The journey of those who have embraced mindfulness illustrates how a calm mind can transform fear into clarity, propelling them toward their goals.

Moreover, community building has become a cornerstone of resilience in entrepreneurship. The realisation that no one is alone in their struggles has inspired many to seek out and create networks of support. Entrepreneurs are increasingly forming alliances with others who share similar experiences, whether through formal networking groups or informal meetups. These connections provide not only emotional support but also practical advice and resources. The personal success stories that emerge from these communities showcase how collective resilience can amplify individual strength, creating a ripple effect of empowerment.

Lastly, the rise of innovative problem-solving approaches marks a significant trend in entrepreneurial resilience. In an era defined by rapid change, entrepreneurs are learning to pivot quickly and adapt their strategies. This agility is rooted in a mindset that embraces experimentation and learning from failures. Entrepreneurs who have faced setbacks often recount how those experiences fueled their creativity and led to unexpected breakthroughs.

Their journeys show that resilience means moving forward and learning from experience. The fearless entrepreneur inspires others to turn fear into action and chase their goals with determination.

Preparing for Future Challenges

Preparing for future challenges requires a proactive mindset, one that embraces uncertainty and views obstacles as opportunities for growth. In the journey of entrepreneurship, fear often lurks in the shadows, ready to paralyse dreams and ambitions. However, by recognising that challenges are an inevitable part of the entrepreneurial landscape, you can shift your perspective. Every successful entrepreneur has faced trials, and it is their ability to adapt and prepare that sets them apart. Embracing a fearless attitude begins with acknowledging that setbacks are not the end of your journey but rather stepping stones to greater achievements.

One effective way to prepare for future challenges is through continuous learning. The most successful entrepreneurs are those who prioritise knowledge acquisition, whether through formal education, mentorship, or self-study. By familiarising yourself with industry trends, market dynamics, and emerging technologies, you equip yourself with the tools necessary to navigate uncertainties. Consider seeking out workshops, webinars, or networking events that inspire you and expand your understanding. The more you learn, the more confident you will become in facing unexpected hurdles, transforming fear into a powerful motivator.

Building a strong support network is another critical element in preparing for future challenges. Surround yourself with like-minded individuals who understand the entrepreneurial journey and can provide encouragement and guidance. Share your experiences, fears, and aspirations with peers, mentors, or even a mastermind group.

These connections not only offer valuable insights but also create a sense of community that can uplift you during hard times. Remember, vulnerability is a strength, and sharing your struggles can forge deeper relationships that enhance your resilience.

Moreover, developing a robust risk management strategy is essential for any entrepreneur. Assess potential risks in your business and create contingency plans that address them. This proactive approach not only minimises potential losses but also instills a sense of control over your circumstances. When you prepare for the unexpected, you can face challenges with a level head and a strategic mindset. This preparation allows you to act rather than react, turning anxiety into informed decision-making that propels your business forward.

Finally, embrace a mindset of adaptability. The entrepreneurial landscape is ever-changing, and those who can pivot in response to challenges will thrive. Cultivating new ideas, changing your approach when necessary, and viewing failure as a chance to learn and grow. Each setback can serve as a lesson, teaching you invaluable skills that will better prepare you for the future.

By fostering resilience and adaptability, you can transform fear into action, empowering yourself to tackle any challenge that lies ahead with courage and determination.

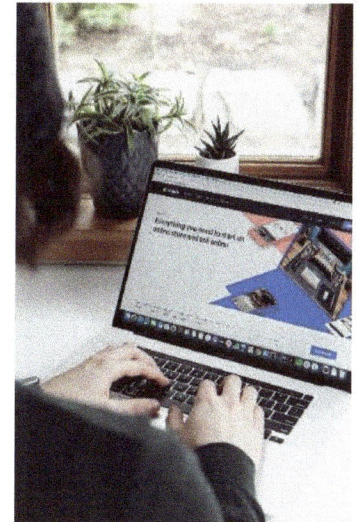

Continuing the Journey Beyond Fear

Continuing the journey beyond fear requires a profound commitment to self-discovery and growth. As entrepreneurs, we often find ourselves at crossroads, where the weight of our fears can feel paralysing. However, it is essential to remember that fear can be a powerful catalyst for change. Embracing this fear rather than shying away from it opens doors to new opportunities and insights.

Each step taken in the face of fear not only builds resilience but also enhances our understanding of what it means to be truly fearless.

Personal success stories demonstrate how individuals have effectively converted their anxieties into constructive action. These accounts offer encouragement and underscore the shared nature of such challenges. For example, one narrative features a young entrepreneur who established her startup while overcoming significant self-doubt.

By confronting her fears head-on—whether through public speaking, networking, or seeking mentorship—she discovered a newfound confidence that propelled her business forward. Her journey exemplifies how confronting fear can lead to unexpected triumphs and personal breakthroughs.

The process of continuing beyond fear involves cultivating a mindset of growth and resilience. Entrepreneurs must learn to view challenges as opportunities to innovate and adapt. This shift in perspective can be transformative. Rather than seeing setbacks as failures, they become stepping stones toward success. By reframing our internal dialogue and embracing vulnerability, we empower ourselves to take calculated risks. This proactive approach not only fosters personal growth but also inspires those around us, creating a ripple effect that encourages others to pursue their own entrepreneurial dreams.

As we navigate the entrepreneurial landscape, it is vital to build a supportive community that understands the complexities of fear. Surrounding ourselves with like-minded individuals who share their own stories of overcoming fear can create an environment of encouragement and motivation. Collaborative efforts can lead to shared resources, accountability, and a sense of belonging. These connections remind us that fear is a universal experience, and together we can forge paths that transcend our limitations.

In continuing the journey beyond fear, we unlock our true potential as entrepreneurs. Each moment spent in discomfort is an investment in our future selves. By embracing fear, we not only pave the way for personal success but also inspire others to embark on their own journeys. The road may be fraught with challenges, but the rewards of resilience, community, and growth are immeasurable. In the end, it is our ability to move forward despite our fears that define our success and shape our legacy as fearless entrepreneurs.

The Fearless Entrepreneur: Transforming anxiety into action

The entrepreneurial journey is often paved with both excitement and anxiety. This is a story of learning to navigate that terrain. The Fearless Entrepreneur shares a deeply personal account of transforming the crippling effects of anxiety into a catalyst for bold action and meaningful achievement in the world of business. Discover the insights and strategies that can help you do the same, turning your fears into greatest strengths.

Notes

Notes

Notes

Notes

Notes